SAP Security Essentials

By SAPCOOKBOOK.COM

SAP Security Essentials

Please visit our website at www.sapcookbook.com
© 2005 Equity Press all rights reserved.

ISBN 1-933804-02-5

Trademark notices

SAP, SAP ERP, SAP SRM, Netweaver, and SAP New Dimension are registered trademarks of SAP AG. This publisher acknowledges SAP permission to use its trademarks in this publication and not the publisher of this book and is not responsible for it under any aspect of the law.

SAP Security Essentials

Motivation

I have found that a of the materials available in SAP security are either 1) nonexistent 2) too general and pedantic in nature 3) sales materials in disguise. And since there are a very limited number of published books in the area of SAP security, this title was a natural addition to our growing library of practical references for SAP consultants and managers.

This book, SAP Security Essentials, started as a list of particularly useful FAQs in the area of SAP security. That is to say, this is a list of tips and tricks that I have used on projects in the past and thought were good enough to include in a book. So for this book, we are calling each tip, trick, recipe, an "essential."

I hope these SAP Security Essentials are as valuable to you as they have been to me.

Introduction

Each security essential has a question (problem), and an answer – that is pretty straightforward – but when you see the guru icon – this is information that represents the highest degree of knowledge and understanding in a particular area. So be aware that to completely understand any given issue, you should read beyond the first answer.

  The Security Guru has Spoken!

75 SAP Security Essentials

Essential 1: Role Naming Procedures

I am trying to determine the best role naming procedures. We are doing a security set-up redesign and would like to use "Generally Accepted Security Role Naming Practices." We are a global company with decentralized SAP set-up with SAP instances for each region.

A: The intent of developing a naming convention for SAP access is to facilitate long-term maintenance of Security, enhance auditing features, and improve the periodic review of access. The following is a proposal for the naming convention guidelines for Roles, Profiles and Authorizations. Note: Composite Role naming conventions are not covered as they are NOT recommended for use.

Naming Conventions: Roles 'Z' or 'Y' is not needed as part of the naming convention. SAP Security is Master Data, not configuration or repository object and therefore does not need the standard development name space. The ':' is the customer designation.

Role name template: xxxx;yyyy_Describe_org. Designate xxxx as major company division, (i.e, Jones, Inc., Parts, etc.). : is the Customer Role designation;

yyyy is the Functional area in SAP such as Financial Accounts Payable (FIAP) or Materials Management Warehouse Maintenance (MMWM).

Under Describe give brief description of Role, i.e., INVOICE_PROCESSOR; Org is any major organizational designations such as plant, sales org or warehouse.

Example: J:FIAP_INVOICE_PROCESSOR is Jones, Inc. Financial Accounts Payable Invoice Processor for the company.

Jones, Inc. is the company, so there is no need to use the _org designation. If this role did ALL or cross company, then a designation would be needed.

Note: If you set the configuration for Session Manager to sort the roles for display, they sort in alphabetical order by technical name. Your generic System roles (Printing, RFC, GUI control, SU56, SU53, SU3, SMX) should sort to the bottom; yyyy should be Cross Application, or XA.

Essential 2: Display Only SM59

SM59 text mentions it can be used for Display/Maintain RFC Connections, how can you make this transaction code display only?

A: SM59 is for Display AND Change. There is no display only version. Sorry, it can't be done.

Essential 3: APO Authorizations

Regarding APO authorizations, can you limit to display only in the product master using transaction code /SAPAPO/MAT1?

A: For the /SAPAPO/MAT1, make sure you have only 03 on C_APO_PROD.

Essential 4: Tcode /SAPAPO/SDP94

In the planning book screen, certain buttons are missing when using tcode /SAPAPO/SDP94. Neither the "Selection Window" nor the "Display Dependant Objects" buttons are visible.

A: Maintain C_APO_FUN to have C_SELCTION, C_SELE and C_SELORG on field APO_FUNC and the name of the planning area on APO_PAREA to make sure /SAPAPO/SDP94 is fully functional and viewable.

Essential 5: Comparing user assignments

How do you compare two user's roles assignments? (i.e., What roles is user FOO missing to have exactly the same roles as user BAR?)

A: In tcode SUIM there is a report to compare users/ roles and selected output.

The best way to make user BAR have the same access as user FOO is to have one role with the access and assign it to each of them once in tcode SU01. Ensure that this is the only role they have.

If this becomes too complicated, use a program to read in the AGR_USERS tables for two users, and lay out the role assignments side by side showing where the role assignment gaps are.

Essential 6: Table names

What is the table name which houses the full list of activities? (01 change, 02, 03 display, etc...)?

A: The table is TACT. Possible activities for one authorized object is: TACTZ.

The list of additional activities is extensive. Go to the profile generator/authorizations screen, pick up any autho object and get to the selection screen for possible activities. Right click and you will see "More values - F7" for a complete list of activities.

Note: May not work for all "activity" fields. In the field for F_REGU_BUK, for example, the values are kept are in a pull-down menu in the transaction F110.

Essential 7: Cost center field in SU01

What is the purpose of the cost center field in the SU01 user master record?

A: It is most likely used to allocate costs of system usage to cost centers. Some use it for internal reporting. It is accessible in some of the ALV reports in SUIM.

Essential 8: Security report scheduling

Are there any periodic security reports that need to be scheduled to monitor during maintenance?

A: Try running user compare -
RHAUTUPD_NEW
SUIM table sync - SUSR_SYNC_USER_TABLES

 Other valuable reports:

USTxx Sync to USRxxx (custom program)

RHPROFL0 (for security by position)

Lock/delete inactive users (custom program)

Delete orphaned authorizations/profile (custom program)

Delete orphaned address info.

RHAUTUPD_NEW

Critical User monitoring report and notification (custom program)

Essential 9: Querying restricted roles

Is it possible to query all roles that have a particular Organizational Level Restriction? (e.g. Company Code, Plant, Division, etc.?)

A: You can get all the roles that have an authorization for a particular object that contain a company code or plant or other authorization value. Those reports are in transaction SUIM.

Essential 10: Accidental deletions

Users in our system were deleted when they shouldn't have been. To determine how this happened, can I retrace the function or is it logged on a table?

A: Debug or use RSUSR100 to find the information.

Essential 11: Accidental deletions 2

While working in development server, my session was deleted by another user. Is there a way to find the user that deleted it, the system number and the related data?

A: Try using TX STAT (or STAD, depends on release) and look for someone who has used TX SM04.

With that, you can kill the session. If more than one user has used the same tcode at the given time, SM21 has the entry logged for it.

You can find who ran SM04 and delete that user's session.

Essential 12: Conflicting combinations

How do you find the typical conflicting combinations of authorization objects in HR, like conflicting tcodes, infotypes and clusters?

A: If you are looking for conflicts within HR, there aren't many. Some companies use security measures to limit payroll information, update disciplinary actions, promotion potential and medical to specific individuals. It is not done with tcodes, but with limited Info types.

SAP HR is written as a central set of tcodes with access limited by data.

The main tcodes are PA40, PA30 and PA20, HR org management is the PA10, PA03, PA13 or the POME and "run Payroll".

Concentrate on the Info types not necessarily the tcodes not objects as they all use P_ORGIN (or what you configure). The only anomaly is P_ABAP which can override P_ORGIN.

Essential 13: The Parameters tab

What is the "Parameters" tab in the SU01 user maintenance screen for?

A: The "Parameters" tab allows users to pre-set entries in order to fill field values in tcodes without having to re-key. Also used for "Set Preferences."

Essential 14: Org Level Tables

Is there a comprehensive list of all the Org Level Tables?

A: Try table AUTHX via SE16.

If it is not loaded or incomplete, use the underlying source structures in SE11, including structures: AUTHA, AUTHB, AUTHC and a few others (search on AUTH*). Look for the Check table or value tables. Note: If AUTHX is not loaded, there is a report to load it.

Essential 15: Setting values in authorization objects

When setting values in an auth obj, is there a way to exclude a specific value without compromising the access of the others?

Example: I'm trying to restrict S_TABU_DIS to allow certain people to see all the auth groups except SS. If someone creates an auth group in the system, we want the people with this role to see the added group without us going back into the role and adding the value via pfcg.

A: Set the values to be included - 00 to SR and ST to ZZ, this would exclude SS.

Essential 16: Authorization reports

How are authorization reports generated? The reports should include activity by object and be accessible to all users with access.

A: Run SUSR_SYNC_USER_TABLES and then try tcode SUIM/report RSUSR002. Enter your object in Object 1 and press enter. Follow the prompts.

Essential 17: Movement types

How do you restrict users on Movement types and certain storage locations in transaction MB1B? The only object displayed in SU24 for MB1B, with a combination of Movement type and Storage location, is M_MSEG_LGO. How do we enable the system to check this object in MB1B? Or, how can we restrict users on a combination of Storage location and Movement type in transaction MB1B?

A: Storage location must be configured to check authorization on each storage location. SAP does not do this by default so there is no ST01 trace of it until you configure it. This is done in the IMG (tcode SPRO).

If you get the help documentation of M_MSEG_LGO (using SU21), there is a link with the correct customizing tcode which turn on/off the authority check on it (under material management-stocks)

This works only for good movements, not for display stocks content.

Essential 18:
Login/disable_multi_gui_login

**Will activating parameter
login/disable_multi_gui_login affect
workflow?**

A: No, the key is the GUI in the parameter.
Workflow does not initiate a GUI logon but a logon
in the "background" or via RFC to a non-GUI
display session.

Note: This parameter is for multiple GUI
logins via the SAP Logon Pad or equivalent.

Essential 19: Expert mode

What is the Expert mode in Profile generation?
What are the options for its use?

A: Expert mode merges existing authorizations with new auths as they are added to the role. The auths display tells you which authorization objects have been added or changed. This is a time-saver in that it clearly lists changes and what to maintain.

 Note: Always work in Expert mode.

Essential 20: Accessing authorization objects

Is there a table where I can access the name of a particular Authorization Object? Possibly a SUIM report?

A: Start with SU24; it will give the objects/transactions in pfcg use.

After SU24 there are tables USOBT_C and USOBX_C.

SU25, Step 1 is mandatory to initialize these tables. Note: Read Help carefully before executing SU25, Step 1.

Essential 21: Display transaction code in PFCG?

How do you display the transaction code in the Menu folder using PFCG?

A: With and existing role, the transactions may be entered straight into the S_TCODE auth object, not the menu.

If the subfolder "Menu" in PFCG displays the list of transactions with only text appearing and not transaction codes, the option needs to be changed.

Go to the right of the screen, beneath the menu tabs and next to the print icon, you will see an icon in the shape of a magnifying glass with either a - or a + symbol in it. Click on that to turn technical names on and off

---

Essential 22: Upgrading issues

What steps to I take to avoid any security issues that might result when upgrading from SAP 4.6c?

A: Run SU25 Steps 2a...2c.

Essential 23: ITAR Issues

Does SAP Security have specific recommendations for maintaining International Traffic in Arms Regulations (ITAR)?

A: Your ITAR restrictions are specific to your company. However, the existing SAP methods of restrictions should work as well, except in the PS module in 4.6C. In that case, some custom modifications to restrict Projects and WBS elements may be needed.

Note: Be sure to keep detailed documentation of your role design, testing and monitor/review plans in the event of a government (DCAA & DCMA) audit.

Essential 24: ABAP Authority check

How is the ABAP AUTHORITY-CHECK statement used?

A: It checks and divulges authority information in SAP reports. You can also access through a search engine by typing "authority-check" ABAP (or similar).

Go to an ABAP program; click once on AUTHORITY-CHECK. Press F1.

Essential 25: Disable billing blocks

How can we disable the Billing Block field on the Sales tab in the Sales Order in VA02, SAP 4.6c?

A: Use V_VBAK_AAT/02.

Essential 26: Disable SPRO

Is it possible to disable customizing (SPRO) for a
certain client while enabling changes in tcode OB52
at the same time?

A: To disable SPRO: Set your client to
"Production" and reset changes to "No Changes
Allowed." OB52 will be maintainable, with the
exception of the tcodes that automatically change
when Production is set.

Note: There may be some variance in
older versions; in that case, use SOBJ to update
your OB52 setting.

Essential 27: Restricting access from MM03

How can we restrict access to the "Current" and "Previous" buttons from the MM03 Costing 2 tab?

A: Set authorization groups on BOM; this should block those without display access. The authorization group field must be populated for the BOM

Essential 28: Creating new CATT in 6.4

Can you create a new catt in 6.4? I get a message to use ecatt instead. I created the test script but cannot figure out the variant.

My thought is to create a variant for export. I could populate the fields in the text file and run the test config that runs that script and updates user i.d.'s.

A: You need to define recording parameters. Create a data container with the same parameters and input your values. To execute, use the test configuration to combine the test script and data container together.

Essential 29: Changing doc types

A user needs to change a doc type 001 for auth group 1; another needs to display doc type 002 for auth group 2. Currently, they can change and display both.

A: If there is an auth group for each doc type and you want to change and display in one role, you need to copy the object in the role (Edit->copy authorizations). In one object put change activity for auth group 1, in the other object put display for auth group 2.

This will create two authorizations which will be evaluated independently of each other

Essential 30: Transaction code access

We have a user that is able to run every transaction code. I've checked the profile in SU01 (not SAP_ALL) and all the roles for this user, but I couldn't locate the tcode. How can I find the error?

A: Has a manual profile been given to that user? You may find the authorization for the tcode in there. If not, use SUIM to filter out your selection.

Look in UST04 to see what profiles the user has. There may be a strange entry for a tcode object in UST10C in the field BIS.

Run Report RSUSR060 (where used - for auth values).
Then search for obj S_TCODE for a value of all transactions '*' by profile.

Your user should be assigned to one of these.

Essential 31: Authorization object V_VBAK_VKO

How can I create a customized table for data maintenance allowing access only for user controlled by sales area level using authorization object V_VBAK_VKO?

We won't give SM30 to the user, so I have created a new tcode for the customized table.

A: You have a few options:

Create a customized program.

Use parameterized tcode to table (see tcode OB52 as an example). It only controls the auth group you add to the table through SE11, SUCU or SE54.

Create the customized program and add S_TABU_LIN configuration to control access to a field in the table.

Essential 32: Accidental auth objects

Inadvertently, we created a handful of custom auth objects that we did not want in SAP_ALL. They were added automatically; how can I remove them?

A: Maintain the profiles in the profile generator Tx PFCG.

Use SM30 to maintain PRGN_CUST. Add entry: ADD_ALL_CUST_OBJECTS. Blank is the default value = 'YES'; change it to 'NO'.

Essential 33: Tracking user data

How do we track data being accessed by a specific user? (i.e., we need to know who is accessing, viewing or maintaining, certain employee payroll data.) Is there a log report for this?

A: HR data access can be seen via the change document reports in HR; viewing may be impossible.

ST03 and STAT will tell you what reports and what SE16 tables were accessed.

Essential 34: Changing user defaults

How can allow a central user to change user defaults and parameters for other users without allowing full-access to SU01?

We currently authorize users to change their own settings with SU50 and SU2, but we haven't figured out a way to do this without opening up access to maintain user roles and profiles, which we do not allow.

A: You can do this by allowing access to SU01, but not giving S_USER_AGR or S_USER_PRO. That way no roles or profiles can be assigned, but all other data can be maintained (name, address, email etc). You can further limit what user groups access is granted for via S_USER_GRP. This may cause issues in a productive environment; test thoroughly before executing.

S_TCODE <OBJ> Authorization check for transaction start
TCD <FLD> Transaction code
SU01
S_USER_GRP <OBJ> User Master Maintenance: User Groups
ACTVT <FLD> Activity
02
03
CLASS <FLD> User group in user master maintenance

Essential 35: Changing auth group names

I need to change the authorization group names for a large number of tables. What should I protect against when doing that? I plan to work in DEV boxes, transport to QA and to live.

A: Make sure your roles are adjusted to the new auth grp values before the changes go live. Users probably won't even notice. You can use some tables in your preparation: Table TDDAT can be used to see all the tables that have a certain auth group.

Table TBRG for object S_TABU_DIS will give you all the auth grps allocated to a table controlled by this object.

Tables and their auth group can be seen in tcode SE54 and SUCU as well. Table TBRG only has the "documented auth groups." You can use what you want and they do not have to be in the table TBRG

Essential 36: Authorizing hierarchies

Is it possible to authorize hierarchies in transaction code UCMON in SEM-BW? I need to prevent the display of the entire hierarchy when a user is not authorized for it. I can authorize the activities, but users can see the entire tree/subtree of all hierarchies that have been created.

A: If your users are only displaying data, they should do it in bex analyzer, which prevents them from viewing the consolidation monitor. Bex is the ideal mode for controlling the level of hierarchy.

Essential 37: BDC user vs. service user

What is the difference between BDC user and service user?

A: A BDC user is one designed to be used for a BDC session (batch input session) run in batch. A few places SAP check the type of user before it allows the process to complete. SM35 is one; its password does not expire and it cannot be used interactively.

Communication ID is designed to be used in RFC connection defined in SM59. The password does not expire and the id cannot be used in dialog processes.

A BDC user ID can be used in SM59 RFC but a Communication ID (CPIC) cannot be used in a BDC session.

SAP Security Essentials

Essential 38: RESPAREA

Previously, RESPAREA has been made an org-level. When viewing the object in the org-level it shows that there is access to HI, KN, KS, PC and PH.

Our customer is having a problem in KO04. A trace shows that it fails on RESPAREA with OR in K_ORDER. When looking at RESPAREA in the object itself I can see OR as an option, but not in the org-level.

How can I include OR in RESPAREA in the org-level?

A: Try Note 565436.

Essential 39: HR go-live

We are preparing for an HR go-live with structural authorization applied. We have the following business requirement:

A user has 1 centralized OM and PA display roles (the whole organization). This user will also need a PA admin role that we have created, with a structural profile that limits access to a specific ORG unit.

If I assign all three roles to this user, the result is that he will have the combined access of all three roles, however he will only be able to view the entire ORG through his OM and PA display roles because the structural profile will restrict him to the single ORG unit overall.

Is there any way to have structural profiles apply differently for each role?

My goal is to allow this user to view the entire ORG via his OM and PA display roles and maintain (i.e., PA30) only specified ORG units via a PA Admin role and structural restriction.

A: In standard SAP probably not. There is a change you can use in the function module option on the structural authorization to get it to do what you want. The other option, if you are in the correct version, is to look at the new objects in HR, called contexts, that allow you to assign the PD profile to the authorization (role) and it may accomplish what you want.

One other check is to see if the org management tcodes check object P_ABAP, (use ST01 authorization trace). If it does you can make it program specific so it bypasses the other checks for that program only.

The context solution works well but is only applicable to PA and not OM (i.e. no context for OM related objects).

The P_ABAP solution only switches off infotype checks, not structural auths, and only for reporting of items running through logical databases SAPDBPNP/ SAPDBPAP.

There is a document on service.sap.com, called "context sensitive realization of the authorization check in HR master data" which covers functionality. It should solve most of your issues, depending on how complicated your system is.

Essential 40: Field values in auth groups

I have a Essential regarding authorization groups. When we give field values for authorization objects have a field named authorization groups, (i.e., in object mm_mate_wgr, a field for authorization group is given).

How can we create these authorization groups? Is there a tcode or another way to do it?

A: You don't have to create the field codes, but you can if you want. You can enter an arbitrary 4 character string and as long as it matches with the one you have put on the corresponding data set then it will work.

If you want to know how to set them up so you will get a drop down list, run a search to get a few detailed posts about the steps you need to take.

M_MATE_WGR

Enter something in the authorisation group field in the basic data material master view.

Give users access to the auth group in their role for this M_MATE_WGR object.

Essential 41: CCMS Configuration

I get a logon error. which reads: Logon failed; Call of URL http://<xi-system>:8000/sap/bc/bsp/sap/spi monitor/monitor.do terminated due to error in logon data.

A: First, check the validity of your SSO ticket for this system. If you do not have a user ID, contact your system administrator.

Error Code: ICF-LE-http-c:100-l:E-T:21-C:3-U:5-P:5-L:7

HTTP 401 - Unauthorized

If the user ID and password are correct; it may be an authorization issue.

If you are using 6.40 WAS, double-check your input. In the higher releases, passwords are case sensitive for non-ABAP to ABAP.

Essential 42: FICO SME

I have a FICO SME attempting to set the Auth Group in the above object to a specific value, say 0001 for display only and he negative tested and put in the value in the testid of 0002 and it passed when it should have failed. He did the SU53 but got the "successful auth check" message. This should not have happened according to our security field settings.

The SME is attempting to restrict users to particular auth groups when displaying report groups. Again this does not seem to work. When he adds a group to the auth group for the G_801K_GLB object, it allows access. I ran a trace and it is not even checking the object. The object is checked but not check maintain. How can we resolve?

A: You may have found a technically empty shell concept and you will need to look for a different control object. Your last resort is S_PROGRAM; but you will need a concept first.

It's possible that you're expecting the object to work in a way it is not intended. The object controls who can change the layout, not use it. There should be another set of G_xxx that are used to control use of the layout. If the auth group is blank, (it is not showing up in the trace) see if the documentation in SU21 for the object can help.

Essential 43: Self-service password reset

Is there a self-service tool with which end-users can reset their passwords themselves? I imagine a function call with a web surface would be quite effective. Does anyone have some code/tool to sell?

A: The Standard Tool should allow for user authentication against LDAP/RACF password, determine if user is locked or not in SAP (and if administrator locked - disallow unlock), reset password and send email to user with new password.

Essential 44: Transaction VF02

I want to prevent users releasing billing documents to accounting in transaction VF02. The activity to release is 43, but this activity is not assigned to the authorization objects for this transaction.

A: Open the activity selection screen for a given authorization object.
Left click > Select "More Values"
All activities as listed in table TACT will appear for selection.
If you are still having problems, hit the F7 key on your keyboard in the Activity dialog box - this will show all available ACTVT values, regardless of whether they relate to the object.

Essential 45: Remote copy

We did a remote client copy from PRD (Source) to DEV (Target) selecting SAP_USER profile.

The remote copy was successful but we are unable to see the basic maintenance and complete views in the target client's PFCG transaction. Are there any settings that can get both?

A: In transaction PFCG, go to the top menu bar. Under utilities there is an option for the whih view you need.

Essential 46: Surveying departments

We are in the implementation phase of SAP, and I have been assigned the task to taking a survey and notating the users in all departments (modules) for our SAP User Licenses.

What is the easiest way to prepare user lists? (It was very difficult to get an overview of users.)

A: Create user groups to categorize the users with transaction SUGR. This makes for simple reporting through SUIM.

Note: Use USMM to display current license classifications and assign accordingly.

Essential 47: Op SAP PS

We have set op SAP PS for use in two company codes/plants.

We want to set authorizations in such a way that staff in one cc cannot write time on networks in the other cc, but so far have not been able to find a solution for this.

We are using CATS for timewriting and have 2 separate WBS structures in each cc, with some WBS elements in cc A to a project in cc B.

We want to ensure that people in cc A do not write time on networks in cc B.

A: Are you referring to CATS and not performing scheduling on the projects? If it's CATS limitations you're looking for, you would need to explore the CATS user exits. Test carefully; CATS is very temperamental and you are potentially impacting a large number of users that would be/could be attempting to charge to a project.

Exit to consider:
CATS0006 CATS: Validate entire time sheet

If you're looking at limiting network restrictions within PS functionality, use:

CNEX0002
EXIT_SAPLCNAU_003 PS Customer Exit Network Header Auth Check

EXIT_SAPLCNAU_004 PS Customer Exit Network Activity Auth Check

These same exits can be called from non-PS transactions, particularly PM, since networks are a form of order (shared by PM, QM, CO ....). Again, know what you're doing and test carefully.

By activating these exits, and not even adding code, you'll find you've brought the logistics modules to a stand still until you've added at least one line of code to them for SAP_X_ACTVT - returning a value of 'X'.

Essential 48: Transaction execution

Is there a way I can find out which transactions a particular user used on a certain day?

A: Use STAT for up to 24 +/- hours; ST03 or ST03N for up to a week. After that, it gets summarized to weekly and monthly data.

Essential 49: Auth object f_lfa1_grp

Can auth object f_lfa1_grp be used in TRANSACTION level?

It works in XK01/FK01 (create vendor) but not in FV60/F-43.

A: This is a master data control object. Use authorization groups and F_BKPF_BEK to have group specific control at the transaction level.

Essential 50: Query group in QuickViewer

We have secured SAP queries based on Query Group. However, when a query is created using QuickViewer, then converted to a SAP query for use by others, it encounters an authorization failure because the user does not have S_TABU_DIS display access for the authorization group of the underlying table.

Without knowing every query in the query group and every table assigned to the query group, how do we give access to this query?

A: There is no way without analyzing each Quick Viewer and each table it uses and then referencing TDDAT table for the auth groups.

If you use PFCG's option to "add a report" (as opposed to "add a transaction") and have PFCG create the transaction code, you will not need to use the user groups at all.

You can configure SU24 with the tcode PFCG creates to all the S_TABU_DIS requirements, so when the tcode is added to any role you will not have to recreate the access each time.

Some prefer to avoid user groups for queries by adding the generated report (not the query) to a report tree or role, which helps avoid all the user group pitfalls.

Essential 51: Critical combinations

Is there a report in SAP that can show all the critical combinations of transactions assigned to a user? (I tried a report in SUIM but it needs the table SUKRI to access the list of critical combinations.) Is there another route to finding a list of the possible critical combinations?

A: You can run RSUSR008 for tcode combination but it will not tell you if the user can complete the tcodes. RSUSR009 can be configured to show conflicting access based on the authorizations needed to complete the business processes.

In higher versions there is a RSUSR008_009_NEW that allows you to define business processes so the results are easier to determine.

A few matrices have been posted in the forums over the last couple of years - you may want to search for these. You could get some generic info from these sites: http://www.auditnet.org/ - you may need to register. http://www.sapbasis.org/securitydocs.htm

Note: Prior to running these programs, determine what your company considers "critical" or you will yield a great deal of work for extraneous information.

Essential 52: Creating a role in SAP CRM

I am creating a role in SAP CRM with transaction PPOCA_CRM : Creation of New org unit.

Once I add the transaction to the role, I can't see transaction code but get Description "Create org Model" instead. How can I view the codes from the role which were added?

A: In the menu part of the role, there is a + sign; click on that and you will see transaction + description.

Essential 53: Specialized login problems

I am not able to login into PRD server using SAP* login and DDIC login. I also tried with default password of these ids also. (06071992,19920706,PASS). Our seniors set the password for these ids and were later resigned. I am not able to find the original passwords.

Some experts in this site told to execute the below query and try to login again:

Before executing the 'Delete sapr3.usr02 where bname = 'sap*' and mandt = '122';', I want to run the select query for this.

While executing the following query in OS level, I get the error message: "table or view does not exist."

pmldev:devadm 1>sqlplus /nolog
SQL>connect /as sysdba;
Connected.
SQL>select bname from sapr3.usr02 where bname = 'sap*' and mandt = '122';
select bname from sapr3.usr02 where bname = 'sap*' and mandt = '122'
*
ERROR at line 1:
ORA-00942: table or view does not exist
SQL>

A: If this system was installed with version 4.7, you must use a schema owner:
Select bname from sap[SID].usr02 where bname = 'sap*' and mandt = '122';

Essential 54: Executing ST03

I am attempting to execute ST03 and am unable to find the usage history in enterprise version. Once I execute, I do not know how to proceed.

A: Use SE11 to understand what ST03 used, then use SE11 again to help yourself to find what is new /changing.

Essential 55: Turning off modify data

I would like to recommend our BASIS person turn off the modify data value of variables during debug mode in our production system to avoid accidental direct debugging table updates and integrity problems.

How can we implement this security profile so that it can only be given to certain individuals?

A: Debug with replace S_DEVELOP activity (ACTVT) = 02 and OTYPE = 'DEBUG' - all other fields are blank (represented by single-quote-space-single-quote)

You can also update debug with 03 in older releases/ level if you can submit a program in update task.

You can also globally deactivate normal debugging in higher releases via a control of the debugger session from the dispatcher.

You will get a message stating "Debugging is impossible at the moment - Please try again later."

Essential 56: Cross module roles

I have a problem with a user who is working in both HR and EHS, so needs a cross module combination of roles.

We have created a custom auth object for P_ORGIN for the HR roles and it is working the way it should.

However, when we combine the EHS with the HR role, the user is missing IT0002 for all subtypes. We want this user restricted to Subtype 9 in the HR role but want the user to view all subtypes in EHS transactions.

Currently the user can only view the users who are in subtype 9 in any of the EHS transactions. Is there a way around this?

When we give the user access to IT0002 for all subtypes, the EHS transactions show all employees and all the HR transactions the user is also able to see all employees which should not happen. The user should only see employees who are in subtype 9 in PA20/PA30.

A: Try OSS Note: 508254 EHS-IHS Authorization check for HR data.

Essential 57: Role FBL3N

I have created a role with FBL3N as its sole transaction and limited it to an authorization group "AA" for GL accounts.

I have added an entry to TBRG for auth obj F_SKA1_BES and given it a value of "AA." I have also changed one GL account to have an auth group of "AA."

However, when I logon as my new user with the FBL3N role, I cannot see the GL account line items for the account that has been given "AA."

I know that the FBL3N role is working because I can see other accounts which have no auth group attached.

A: Run a ST01 authorization trace. Manually add authorization group F_BKPF_BES into the role and limit it to "AA." Add this entry to TBRG and everything should work.

Essential 58: Object F_IT_ALV

What is the benefit of object F_IT_ALV? I am interested in activity 70 (administer) and would like know what it does exactly and what access does the user get if the activity is set to 70?

A: Activity 70 gives users the ability to administer layouts in transactions like FBL1N & FBL3N. This should be restricted to prevent users altering layouts used by other users.

(From the Help Text): Object F_IT_ALV controls the availability of functions for layout maintenance in the ALV list for the line item display. This authorization is optional. If it has not been maintained for a user, it does not affect previous functions. That is, all layout functions are still available without restrictions.

Defined fields

Object F_IT_ALV has a field, activity ACTVT, that can have one of four values: 01, 02, 03 and 70. Each of the activities 01, 02 and 70 specifically controls the availability of a function (in the menu or application toolbar) in the ALV line item list:
01: "Settings -> Display variant -> Save"

02: "Settings -> Display variant -> Current .." and "Settings -> Display variant -> Current header items"
70: "Settings -> Display variant -> Administration"

Activity 03 is the minimum, most restricted authorization: The user can only select preconfigured layouts. All other functions are inactive for activity 03.

If, for example, you want a user to be able to change the column selection and the header items and save this new layout, but do not want him to administrate the layout, then you would give this user authorization for activities 01 and 02.

For more information, see note 374656.

Essential 59: Transaction PV7I

We have an employee trying to book a training from transaction PV7I by pressing "Request Attendance." The system has the message "You have no authorization for the function or the object." When I check the SU53 it said "All authorization checks have so far been successful."

Are there any other tools to prove that this user is authorized or is their some other way to circumvent?

A: On rare occasions, SAP performs a simulation of authorization checks. Thus, no SU53 is present but the user is not authorized. In some cases the error message is wrong.

Note: Try debugging the code and breakpoint a message to find where and what is causing the failure.

Essential 60: Building roles in PFCG

When I want to build a role in PFCG, how can I exclude objects like IS-Beverage and IS-Real Estate objects from appearing in PFCG? Is it in SU22 or SU24?

A: You can exclude an authorization object via SU22/4.

It is recommended to "inactivate" the object in a given role.

Essential 61: Management roles

Change management for roles when I go to SUIM - change documents - roles the values for "old value" and "new value" are blanks.

This is the case for many roles.

Why is the change management for roles not activated?

A: Set the "from date" to a date in the past and select "All Change Documents (Technical View)".

Essential 62: User comparison

Is there any way that the user comparison can be automated? Currently, we manually compare the roles. I have heard that a parameter change will do the trick.

A: Use transaction code SUIM > Comparisons > From Users

Note: Schedule RHAUTUPD_NEW to run periodically.

Essential 63: List personnel areas

Is there is a table, program or a transaction code to run for a list of personnel areas that have been created for HR?

A: Try table T500P

Essential 64: Transaction codes FS00/FSP0

Our supervisors have requested that transaction codes FS00 (G/L Account) and FSP0 (G/L Account in chart of accts) be made display only. This would not be a problem as I could set the Activity to 03.

However, they need users to create and change access to transaction FSS0 which uses the same objects as FS00 and FSP0. Do you know of any way to make the above two transaction codes display only?

Is there a way to assign another display only object to these transactions that would not be checked by FSS0?

A: It is best to give transactions a standard display only tcode and separate the roles.

Reconsider your design and challenge the requirement by changing the tcode. Your company should not request tcodes, but rather a requirement. Give them something to click on and it does not matter what it is called.

You can change the auth checks a little bit with Se93 (at start) and using SU24 check indicators. Hardcoded checks, if reacted to, are the only real checks.

Use the authorization concept to grant auths, depending on whether you want to achieve display or change. Generally, you activate 03 or 02.

Solution may be a combination of both: "What did SAP check?" AND "what did the user have?" (Sometimes the "How did SAP react to the check?" also plays a role.)

Essential 65: Assigned role in child system

How do I find what role I assigned to a user in the child system?

I ran report "display change documents for role administration" via transaction SU01 but it only shows the roles of the CUA system.

A: Just go into the target (child) system and use the table AGR_USERS.

SE16 -> AGR_USERS

Change the "From date" in "Change Documents for Role Assignment" from the current date to a date in the past.

Or, from SU01, you can select "Change Documents for Users." The report will show you the deleted profiles.

The above report with table AGR_PROF will allow you to see the relation between a profile and a role. There are few steps involved, but this will provide you the wanted result.

Essential 66: Db-tab TCURR

Our users must be authorized to change entries in the db-tab TCURR.

We are in SPRO; what do I have to do to authorize?

A: TCURR is maintained via tx OB08. You need to restrict this + change access to S_TABU_DIS auth group FC32.

Essential 67: Executable transactions

How do we find out the executable transactions within multiple roles at one time?

A: Put them all in a user id and execute transx RSUSR010.

Note: In lower versions, RSUSR010 may not warrant the results you need, but in higher versions it will tell you if the user has S_TCODE and the auth object tied to the tcode defined in SE93. It will not tell you if the user can complete the tcode or if the user has access to run a business function executed by a CALL TRANSACTION within another tcode.

RSUSR009 (or the new one), configured correctly, can provide you a more accurate result.

Essential 68:
PHAP_SEARCH_PA

I restrict employee access by creating a personnel area role. However, when user executes transaction PHAP_SEARCH_PA the report generates a list of data from the entire personnel base.

What is wrong? Could it be the report doesn't have an authorization check through Query?

A: Run a ST01 authorization check to see what has been checked. If the report is based on a Logical Data Base it may be checking P_ABAP which overrides the P_ORGIN check.

Essential 69: Restrict Report Variant access

How can I restrict access to edit the Report Variant of others? Is it possible?

A: Yes, when you go to save the variant, click the box that says "Protect Variant." Once the field Protect Variant is selected, it can only be changed by the person who created or last changed it.

Note: If a user has access to report RSVARENT, they may be able to access and/or modify the report.

Essential 70: Overwrite user authorizations

I have created a few users with a set of authorization and roles. These users' names are already in use. I would like to overwrite the authorization of the users by copying roles and profiles of another user without deleting the existing users.

A: Remove the existing roles in SU01 and replace with those you want to want to copy from the access form.

Essential 71: Restrict ME21

We want to restrict tcodes ME21n based on Item Category , but there is no object where we can specify item category field value. We tried to set the trace , the it does not show any object that has item category as field for any object

Users can select item type inside the tcode me21n. What can be done to restrict based on the item category?

A: You can include additional authorization check in the ABAP (User Exit).

Steps:

Search for an already existing authorization object, which might fit.

If such an authorization object does not exist, create a customized authorization object.

Include the authorization object into a User Exit.

Assign the authorization object to the transaction via SU24.

Regenerate the impacted role in expert mode.

Essential 72: Content repository

I am trying to create and configure a Content Repository (transaction OAC0) so I can use my own Content Server with ArchiveLink. When I try to save my configuration, I get the message, "User DDIC may not make changes in Customer systems."

A: Try another i.d. and the user a_ch2005 without SAP_ALL.

You are getting this message because the DDIC user has limited create & change access in SAP.

You should not use DDIC for these tasks.

However, DDIC is required for certain installation and setup tasks in the system, so you should not delete it.

Essential 73: Download list of all SAP transactions

How can I run a report to generate a list of all SAP transactions? I know I can view a list from SE93 and SM01, but I need to download a full list.

A: Try table TSTC for a list of transactions. The texts are in TSTCT.

Essential 74: Finding tables

I have assigned roles to positions. What tables is
this data held in?

A: There is a relationship in IT1001. Try table
HRT1001 (it may be or in conjunction with
HRP1001).

In older versions, it is IT1016

 In 4.6C, we use HRP1001.

Object type = S
Rel.Obj.Type = AG
ID Rel.Obj = your role name

You can play with the other fields (end date, etc) if
needed.

Essential 75: User authorizations

I need to provide authorization for read only of a database table and to other users read and inset/update rights.

What type of user authorizations do I need to build into the code?

A: If you want to restrict the tables in SE12/16/17, you can do that via an authorization group: Assign group to the table and use the authorization object S_TABU_DIS. Coding shouldn't be required.

If you want to provide the authorization access via a program: Use a transaction table to be populated through the program.

Note: Only users with specific access/authorization should populate it.

SM30 (Or create a tcode in SE93 and call SM30 with skipscreen option); Use S_TABU_DIS to search values (see SU21).

Activity 03 = display
Activity 02 = change (etc.)

Use S_TABU_DIS (tode SUCU) to DESIGN what you want to achieve.
Use SU24 / PFCG etc to CONTROL it.

OSS Notes, Tables, and Transaction Codes

SAP R/3 Enterprise OSS Notes

SAP Software Installation

[580341]	SAP Software on UNIX: OS Dependencies 6.30
[520965]	Release restrictions R/3 Enterprise 4.70 / 1.10 Add-Ons
[534334]	Composite SAP note Install./Upgrade? SAP R/3 Enterprise 47x11
[538887]	SAP R/3 Enterprise 47x110: Software Architecture/maintenance
[635608]	Release restrictions for SAP R/3 Enterprise 47x200
[662453]	Composite SAP Note Inst./Upgrade? SAP R/3 Enterprise 47x200
[658351]	SAP R/3 Enterprise 47x200: Software architecture/maintenance
[580341]	SAP Software on UNIX: OS Dependencies 6.30
[534334]	Composite SAP note Installation/Upgrade? SAP R/3
[492222]	SAP Software on UNIX - OS Dependencies
[523505]	SAP R/3 Enterprise Installation Under UNIX
[523502]	INST: SAP R/3 Enterprise 4.7 Inst. Under UNIX - SAP DB
[523503]	INST: SAP R/3 Enterprise 4.7 Inst. Under UNIX - Informix
[523504]	INST: SAP R/3 Enterprise 4.7 Inst. Under UNIX - Oracle
[496251]	INST: SAP Web AS 6.20 on Windows - General
[529151]	SAP R/3 Enterprise Installation UnderWindows? - General
[529076]	INST: SAP R/3 Enterprise 4.7 Under Windows: Oracle
[529118]	INST:SAP R/3 Enterprise 4.7 Under Windows- MS

	Cluster
[529150]	INST:SAP R/3 Enterprise 4.7 UnderWindows?- MS SQL Server
[531349]	INST: SAP R/3 Enterprise 4.7 UnderWindows? - Informix
[531372]	INST: SAP R/3 Enterprise 4.7 Under Windows - SAP DB
[533728]	SAP R/3 Enterprise 4.7 Inst. Under UNIX - IBM DB2 UDB for UNIX and Windows
[533715]	SAP R/3 Enterprise 4.7 Inst. Under Windows 2000 - IBM

System Copy

[547314]	FAQ: System Copy procedure
[89188]	R/3 System copy
[489690]	CC INFO: Copying large production clients
[407123]	INST: SAP Web AS 6.10 - Hom. + Het. System Copy
[516246]	INST: System Copy for SAP Systems based on SAP Web AS 6.20
[677447]	INST: System Copy for SAP Systems based on SAP Web AS 6.30

SAP Business Warehouse

Upgrade

[658992]	Additional information for the upgrade to BW 3.50
[662219]	Add. info. on upgrading to SAP Web AS 6.40 ORACLE

Installation

[552914]	SAP BW 3.1 Content Server Installation on UNIX
[492208]	INST: SAP Web AS 6.20 Installation on UNIX
[492221]	INST: SAP Web AS 6.20 Inst. on UNIX - Oracle
[492222]	SAP Software on UNIX: OS Dependencies 6.20
[421795]	SAP_ANALYZE_ALL_INFOCUBES report
[355814]	Demand Planning: You must work in client 001
[192658]	Setting basis parameters for BW Systems

Internet Graphics Service (IGS)

[458731]	Internet Graphics Service: Main Note
[525716]	6.20: IGS Buglist (and solutions)
[548496]	Overview of IGS Notes (6.20)
[514841]	Troubleshooting when a problem occurs with the IGS
[480692]	SAP IGS support strategy
[443430]	HW/SW Requirements for Internet Graphics Service
[454042]	IGS: Installing and Configuring the IGS

Internet Transaction Server (ITS)

| [721993] | ITS updates in Release 6.40 (SAP Integrated ITS). |

BW System Administration

[428212]	Update of statistics of InfoCubes with BRCONNECT
[150315]	BW-Authorizations for Remote-User in BW and OLTP
[46272]	Implement new data class in technical settings
[371413]	DB data class and size catgory for aggregate tables
[156727]	Default data class for InfoCubes and dimensions
[123546]	Extending the permitted size categories
[443767]	Size category for fact and dimension tables (InfoCube)
[639941]	TABART(Table space) for PSA tables
[550669]	Compressed transfer of BW Web Applications
[561792]	Client-sided caching of image/gif files
[130253]	Notes on upload of transaction data into the BW
[417307]	Extractor package size: Collective note for applications

Oracle

RAC

[527843]	Oracle RAC support in the SAP environment
[581320]	FAQ: Oracle Real Application Cluster (RAC)
[621293]	Oracle9i: Real Application Clusters

Installation

[619188]	FAQ: Oracle Wait Events
[619876]	Oracle9i: Automatic PGA Memory Management
[601157]	Dynamic parameter changes - SPFILE
[145654]	Installing SAP Systems on UNIX/Oracle? with raw devices
[617416]	Oracle9i: Dynamic SGA
[598678]	Composite SAP Note: New functions in Oracle 9i
[180605]	Oracle database parameter settings for BW
[632556]	Oracle 9.2.0.* database parameterization for BW
[632427]	Oracle 8.1.7* database parameterization for BW
[565075]	Recommendations for BW systems with Oracle 8.1.x
[567745]	Composite note BW 3.x performance: DB-specific setting
[359835]	Design of the temporary tablespace in the BW System
[387946]	USE OF LOCALLY MANAGED TABLESPACES FOR BW SYSTEMS
[351163]	Creating ORACLE DB statistics using DBMS_STATS

Administration

[592393]	FAQ: Oracle
[588668]	FAQ: Database statistics
[666061]	FAQ: Database objects, segments and extents
[541538]	FAQ: Reorganizations
[647697]	BRSPACE - New tool for Oracle database administration
[600141]	Oracle9i: Automatic UNDO Management
[60233]	Oracle rollback segments, more information
[385163]	Partitioning on ORACLE since BW 2.0
[335725]	BW (Oracle): Change/restore standard indexing

Problems

[354080]	Note collection for Oracle performance problems
[323090]	Performance problems due to degenerated indexes
[3807]	RBS problems: ORA-01555, ORA-01628, ORA-01650
[185822]	ora-1555 - cause and action
[568632]	Problems with Disk Storage with temporary tables in BW
[178275]	Bitmap Indexes in Wrong Tablespace
[494852]	Primary index of PSA tables in incorrect tablespace
[547464]	Nologging Option when creating indexes
[442763]	Avoid NOLOGGING during the index structure (Oracle)
[159779]	Problems with BITMAPINDEX under ORACLE in BW
[631668]	DEADLOCK when loading data into InfoCubes?
[634458]	ODS object: Activation fails - DEADLOCK
[84348]	Oracle deadlocks, ORA-00060
[750033]	INITRANS parameter for InfoCube? secondary

	indexes

Backup / Restore / Recovery

[442395]	Descriptions of specific BR messages
[17163]	BRARCHIVE/BRBACKUP messages and codes

Software Logistics (Transport System, Add-Ons & Support Packages)

Transports

[11599]	Reversing transports
[456196]	'Couldn't locate TA information in .../co-files' error

Support Packages

[97620]	OCS Info: Overview of Important OCS Notes
[447925]	OCS: Known problems with Supp. Packages in Basis Rel.6.20
[539867]	BW 3.1 Content: Information about Support Packages
[553527]	Support Packages for the PI_BASIS (Basis Plug-in)
[662441]	Solution Manager Support Packages: Known problems

Add-Ons

[555092]	Installation/upgrade Basis plug-in (PI_BASIS) 2002.2

General System Administration

Tuning

Work Processes

[39412]	How many work processes to configure
[21960]	Several instances/systems on one UNIX computer
[9942]	Max. number of work processes is 40 due to events
[33873]	What do the semaphores mean?

Memory Management

[37537]	Performance increase by shared memory pools.
[78498]	High paging rate on AIX servers, in part. database servers .
[95454]	A lot of extended memory on AIX (32 -bit)
[88416]	Zero administration memory management from 4.0A/NT
[110172]	NT: Transactions with large storage requirements
[33576]	Memory Management (as of Release 3.0C, Unix and NT)
[103747]	Performance: Parameter recommendations for Rel. 4.0 and high
[386605]	SAP memory management for Linux
[649327]	Analysis of memory consumption
[548845]	Internal sessions over 2GB
[425207]	SAP memory management, current parameter ranges

Buffering

[504875]	Buffering number ranges

[678501]	System stoppage, locks on table NRIV
[572905]	Unbuffered number ranges

Background Processing

[16083]	Standard jobs, reorganization jobs

Network

[500235]	Network Diagnosis with NIPING

Web Dispatcher

[538405]	Composite SAP note about SAP Web Dispatcher
[561885]	Generation of URLs (SAP Web Dispatcher/Reverse? Proxy)

SAPOSCOL

[548699]	FAQ: OS collector SAPOSCOL

SAP Remote Services

Service Connection

[91488]	SAP Support Services: Central preparation note
[144864]	SAP Remote Services: Technical preparation
[69455]	Servicetools for Applications ST-A/PI (ST14 & RTCCTOOL)
[207223]	Activating the SAP EarlyWatch? Alert
[160777]	SAP GoingLive/EarlyWatch? Check for a BW System
[309711]	SAP Servicetools Update: Online help
[216952]	Service Data Control Center (SDCC) - FAQ
[539977]	Release Strategy for Solution Tools Plug-In
[597673]	Installation/Upgrade? Solution Tools Plug-In 003C (ST-PI)
[560475]	Frequent questions on the Solution Tool Plug-In
[116095]	Solution Tools Plug-In

SAPGUI

SAPGUI For Windows

Via Citrix / Terminal Server

[200694]	Notes on Sapgui for use via terminal server
[431163]	Troubleshooting Citrix Metaframe Issues
[138869]	SAP GUI on Windows Terminal Server (WTS)

General

[66971]	Supported front end platforms
[26417]	SAPGUI Resources: Hardware and software
[166130]	SAP frontend: Delivery and compatibility
[147519]	Maintenance strategy / deadlines 'SAPGUI'
[203924]	Performance 4.6 - collective note
[203617]	High memory consumption with Easy Access menu

Useful SAP Technical Transaction Codes

Background Processing

RZ01	Job Scheduling Monitor
SM36	Schedule Background Job
SM36WIZ	Job definition wizard
SM37	Overview of job selection
SM37B	Simple version of job selection
SM37BAK	Old SM37 backup
SM37C	Flexible version of job selection
SM39	Job Analysis
SM65	Background Processing Analysis Tool
SMX	Display Own Jobs
RZ15	Read XMI log
SM61	Backgroup control objects monitor
SM61B	New control object management

System Monitoring

SM50	Work Process Overview
SM51	List of SAP Systems
SM66	System wide Work Process Overview
STDA	Debugger display/control (server)
SMMS	Message Server Monitor
RZ02	Network Graphics for SAP Instances
RZ03	Presentation, Control SAP Instances
RZ04	Maintain SAP Instances
RZ06	Alerts Thresholds Maintenance
RZ08	SAP Alert Monitor
SM35	Batch Input Monitoring
RZ20	CCMS Monitoring
RZ21	CCMS Monitoring Arch. Customizing
RZ23	Performance database monitor
RZ23N	Central Performance History
RZ25	Start Tools for a TID
RZ26	Start Methods for an Alert
RZ27	Start RZ20 for a Monitor
RZ27_SECURITY	MiniApp? CCMS Alerts Security
RZ28	Start Alert Viewer for Monitor
ST22	ABAP dump analysis
ST22OLD	Old Dump Analysis

Performance Analysis

STAD	Statistics display for all systems
STAT	Local Transaction Statistics
STATTRACE	Global Statistics & Traces
STUN	Menu Performance Monitor
STo2	Setups/Tune? Buffers
STo3	Performance,SAP Statistics, Workload
STo3G	Global Workload Statistics
STo3N	R/3 Workload and Perf. Statistics
STo4	DB Performance Monitor
STo4N	Database Performance Monitor
STP4	Select DB activities
STo4RFC	MS SQL Server Remote Monitor tools
STo5	Performance trace
STo6	Operating System Monitor
STo7	Application monitor
ST10	Table Call Statistics

General System Administration

SM21	Online System Log Analysis
SM01	Lock Transactions
SM02	System Messages
SM04	User List
SM12	Display and Delete Locks
SM13	Administrate Update Records
SM13T	Administrate Update Records
SM14	Update Program Administration

System Configuration

RZ10	Maintain Profile Parameters
RZ11	Profile Parameter Maintenance
RZ12	Maintain RFC Server Group Assignment

Security

SM18	Reorganize Security Audit Log
SM19	Security Audit Configuration
SM20	Security Audit Log Assessment
SM20N	Analysis of Security Audit Log
SA38PARAMETER	Schedule PFCG_TIME_DEPENDENCY

External Communication

SMGW	Gateway Monitor
SM54	TXCOM Maintenance
SM55	THOST Maintenance
SM59	RFC Destinations (Display/Maintain)

SM59_OLD	Transaction SM59 old (<5.0)
SMQ1	qRFC Monitor (Outbound Queue)
SMQ2	qRFC Monitor (Inbound Queue)
SMQ3	qRFC Monitor (Saved E-Queue)
SMQA	tRFC/qRFC: Confirm. status & data
SMQE	qRFC Administration
SMQG	Distributed QOUT Tables
SMQR	Registration of Inbound Queues
SMQS	Registration of Destinations
SMT1	Trusted Systems (Display <-> Maint.)
SMT2	Trusting systems (Display <->Maint.)
SARFC	Server Resources for Asynchron. RFC
SM58	Asynchronous RFC Error Log

Internet Connectivity

SMICM	ICM Monitor
SMICM_SOS	ICM Monitor
SICF	HTTP Service Hierarchy Maintenance

Spool & Print

SP00	Spool and related areas
SP01	Output Controller
SP01O	Spool Controller
SP02	Display Spool Requests
SP02O	Display Output Requests
SP03	Spool: Load Formats
SP11	TemSe? directory
SP12	TemSe? Administration
SP1T	Output Control (Test)
SPAD	Spool Administration
SPCC	Spool consistency check

CATT Test Tool

ST30	Global Perf. Analysis: Execute
ST33	Glob. Perf. Analysis: Display Data
ST34	Glob. Perf. Analysis: Log IDs
ST35	Glob. Perf. Analysis: Assign CATTs
ST36	Glob. Perf. Analysis: Delete Data
ST37	Glob. Perf. Analysis: Eval. Schema
STW1	Test Workbench: Test catalog
STW2	Test workbench: Test plan

STW3	Test Workbench: Test Package
STW4	Test Workbench: Edit test package
STW5	C maintenance table TTPLA
STWBM	Test Workbench Manager
STWB_1	Test Catalog Management
STWB_2	Test Plan Management
STWB_INFO	Test Workbench Infosystem
STWB_SET	Central Test Workbench settings
STWB_TC	Test Case Management
STWB_WORK	Tester Worklist

Transport System

SE01	Transport Organizer (Extended)
SE03	Transport Organizer Tools
SE06	Set Up Transport Organizer
SE07	CTS Status Display
SE09	Transport Organizer
SE10	Transport Organizer
SEPA	EPS Server: Administration
SEPS	SAP Electronic Parcel Service
STMS	Transport Management System
STMS_ALERT	TMS Alert Monitor
STMS_DOM	TMS System Overview
STMS_FSYS	Maintain TMS system lists
STMS_IMPORT	TMS Import Queue
STMS_INBOX	TMS Worklist
STMS_MONI	TMS Import Monitor
STMS_PATH	TMS Transport Routes

STMS_QA	TMS Quality Assurance
STMS_QUEUES	TMS Import Overview
STMS_TCRI	Display/Maintain Table TMSTCRI
STMS_TRACK	TMS Import Tracking

Add-ons & Support Packages

SAINT	Add-On Installation Tool
SPAM	Support Package Manager

ABAP Development

SE11	ABAP Dictionary
SE11_OLD	ABAP/4 Dictionary Maintenance
SE12	ABAP/4 Dictionary Display
SE12_OLD	ABAP/4 Dictionary Display
SE13	Maintain Technical Settings (Tables)
SE14	Utilities for Dictionary Tables
SE15	ABAP/4 Repository Information System
SE21	Package Builder
SE24	Class Builder
SE29	Application Packets
SE30	ABAP Objects Runtime Analysis
SE32	ABAP Text Element Maintenance
SE32_OLD	ABAP Text Element Maintenance
SE32_WB99	ABAP Text Element Maintenance
SE33	Context Builder
SE35	ABAP/4 Dialog Modules
SE36	Logical Database Builder
SE37	ABAP Function Modules

SE38	ABAP Editor
SE38L	SE38 with RCIFIMAX
SE38M	Define Variant for RAPOKZFX
SE38N	SE38 with Default RDELALOG
SE41	Menu Painter
SE43	Maintain Area Menu
SE43N	Maintain Area Menu
SE51	Screen Painter
SE54	Generate table view
SE55	Internal table view maintenance call
SE56	internal call: display table view
SE57	internal delete table view call
STYLE_GUIDE	Style Guide Transaction

Archiving

ALINKVIEWER	ARCHIVELINKVIEWER
ALVIEWER	ArchiveLink? Viewer in the Web
RZPT	Residence Time Maintenance Tool
ALO1	Determine ASH/DOREX Relationships
SARA	Archive Administration
SARE	Archive Explorer
SAR_DA_STAT_ANALYSIS	Analysis of DA Statistics
SAR_OBJ_IND_CUS	Cross-Archiving-Obj. Customizing
SAR_SHOW_MONITOR	Data Archiving Monitor
SARI	Archive Information System
SARJ	Archive Retrieval Configurator

Unsorted

AL02	Database alert monitor
AL03	Operating system alert monitor
AL04	Monitor call distribution
AL05	Monitor current workload
AL08	Users Logged On
AL11	Display SAP Directories
AL12	Display table buffer (Exp. session)
AL13	Display Shared Memory (Expert mode)
AL15	Customize SAPOSCOL destination
AL16	Local Alert Monitor for Operat.Syst.
AL17	Remote Alert Monitor f.Operat. Syst.
AL18	Local File System Monitor
AL19	Remote File System Monitor
ALM99	JBALMCTRL Control Tables
ALM_01	ALM: Assign CF Type to CF Indicator
ALM_02	ALM Sim. Type: Maintain Parameters
ALM_04	Create Planning Variant
ALM_ME_GENERAL	Smartsync Settings
ALM_ME_GETSYNC	Display Synchronization Status
ALM_ME_INVENTORY	Inventory Management Profile
ALM_ME_NOTIF	Notification Processing Profile
ALM_ME_ORDER	Order Processing Profile

ALM_ME_ORDER_STATUS	Change Mobile Status for Order
ALM_ME_SCENARIO	Mobile Asset Management Scenario
ALM_ME_USER	User-specific settings
ALRTCATDEF	Define Alert Category
RZ70	SLD Administration
RZAL_ALERT_PROXY	Alerts: IMC Data Proxy for Alerts
RZAL_MONITOR_PROXY	Alerts: IMC Data Proxy for Monitor
RZAL_MTE_DATA_PROXY	Alerts: IMC Data Proxy for MTEs
SA01	Number range maintenance: ADRNR
SA02	Academic Title (Bus. Addr. Services)
SA03	Titles (Business Address Services)
SA04	Name Prefixes (Bus. Addr. Services)
SA05	Name Suffix (Bus. Address Services)
SA06	Address or personal data source
SA07	Address Groups (Bus. Addr. Services)
SA08	Person Groups (Bus. Addr. Services)
SA09	Internat. versions address admin.
SA10	Address admin. communication type
SA11	Number range maintenance: ADRV
SA12	Number range maintenance:

	ADRVP
SA13	Name format rules
SA14	Pager Services (Bus. Addr. Services)
SA15	Address screen variants
SA15V	Version-Specific Address Templates
SA16	Transport zones
SA17	Duplicate check index pools
SA18	Titles (Business Address Services)
SA19	Titles (Business Address Services)
SA20	Conversion of Street Sections
SA21	Customizing Regional Structure (BAS)
SA22	Deactivate Specific Corrections
SA23	Reg. Structure for Address Versions
SA38	ABAP Reporting
SA39	SA38 for Parameter Transaction
SABPWPFD	Correct Write Protection Violations
SABPWPFDGUI	Write Protection Violation Analysis
SABRE_PNR	Display a Sabre PNR
SAD0	Address Management call
SADC	Address: Maint. communication types
SADJ	Customizing Transfer Assistant
SADP	Contact person addr.maint. init.scr.
SADQ	Private address maint. initial scrn
SADR	Address maint. - Group required!
SADV	International address versions
SAKB0	AKB Configuration
SAKB4	Create Usage Explanations
SAKB5	Check Table Enhancements

SALE	Display ALE Customizing
SALE_CUA	Display ALE Customizing for CUA
SALRT01	Maintain RFC Dest. for Alert Server
SALRT02	Maintain Events for Alert Framework
SALRT1	Maintain RFC Dest. for Alert Server
SAMT	ABAP Program Set Processing
SAPTERM	SAPterm: SAP Dictionary
SARP	Reporting (Tree Structure): Execute
SARPN	Display Report Trees
SART	Display Report Tree
SARTN	Display Report Trees
SASAP01	Implementation Assistant: Display
SASAP02	Implementation Assistant: Scope
SASAPBCS	Call Up BC Sets
SASAPCATT	Call Up CATT
SASAPFLAVOR	Maintain Flavor
SASAPIA	Implementation Assistant: Change
SASA PIAC	Implementation Assistant
SASAPIG	Install.Guide: Authoring Environment
SASAPIGP	Installation Guide:Phase Maintenance
SASAPIMG	Call Up Project IMG
SASAPQADB	Q&&Adb Authoring Environment
SASAPRELS	Maintain Release
SASAPROAD_ROLE	Maintain Roles for ASAP Roadmap
SASAPROAD_SUBJECT	Maintain Subject for ASAP Roadmap
SASAPROLE	Maintain Roles for ASAP

SASAPSUBJECT	Maintain Subject for ASAP
SASAP_IA	ASAP Implementation Assistant
SM28	Installation Check
SM29	Model Transfer for Tables
SM30	Call View Maintenance
SM30_CUS_COUNT	Maintain Table CUS_COUNT
SM30_CUS_INDU	Maintain Table CUS_INDU
SM30_CUS_SYST	Maintain Table CUS_SYST
SM30_PRGN_CUST	Maintain Table SSM_CUST
SM30_SSM_CUST	Maintain Table SSM_CUST
SM30_SSM_EXT	External Node Type Data
SM30_SSM_RFC	Maintain Table SSM_RFC
SM30_SSM_VAR	Maintain Table SSM_VAR
SM30_SSM_VART	variable and text table transaction
SM30_STXSFREPL	Smart Styles: Replace Font
SM30_TVARV	Call SM30 for Table TVARV
SM30_VAL_AKH	Maintain Table VAL_AKH
SM30_VSNCSYSACL	Call Up SM30 for Table VSNCSYSACL
SM30_V_001_COS	Cost of sales accounting status
SM30_V_BRG	Call SM30 for View V_BRG
SM30_V_DDAT	Call SM30 for View V_DDAT
SM30_V_T585A	Call Up SM30 for Table V_T585A
SM30_V_T585B	Call SM30 for Table V_T585B
SM30_V_T585C	Call SM30 for Table V_T585C
SM30_V_T599R	Call Up SM30 for Table V_T599R
SM30_V_TKA05	Cost center categories
SM31	Call View Maintenance Like SM30

SM31_OLD	Old Table Maintenance
SM32	Maintain Table Parameter ID TAB
SM33	Display Table Parameter ID TAB
SM34	Viewcluster Maintenance Call
SM38	Queue Maintenance Transaction
SM49	Execute external OS commands
SM56	Number Range Buffer
SM580	Transaction for Drag & Relate
SM62	
SM63	Display/Maintain? Operating Mode Set
SM64	Trigger an Event
SM69	Maintain External OS Commands
SMAP01	Maintain Solution Map objects
SMARTFORMS	SAP Smart Forms
SMARTFORM_CODE	SAP Smart Forms: Target Coding
SMARTFORM_TRACE	SAP Smart Forms: Trace
SMARTSTYLES	SAP Smart Styles
SMCL	CSL: Monitor
SMEN	Session Manager Menu Tree Display
SMET	Display frequency of function calls
SMETDELBUFF	Del. Measurement data in shared bfr
SMETDELPROG	Delete programs in shared buffer
SMLG	Maint.Assign. Logon Grp to Instance
SMLT	Language Management
SMLT_EX	Language Export

SMME	Output control Message Block Table
SMOD	SAP Enhancement Management
SMOMO	Mobile Engine
SMTR_START_HISTORY	Call object history
SMW0	SAP Web Repository
SMY1	Maintenance of nodes for MyObjects?
SPACKAGE	Package Builder
SPAK	Package Builder
SPAR	Determine storage parameters
SPAT	Spool Administration (Test)
SPAU	Display Modified DE Objects
SPBM	Monitoring parallel background tasks
SPBT	Test: Parallel background tasks
SPDD	Display Modified DDIC Objects
SPEC01	Specification system: Edit template
SPEC02	Specification system: Edit datasheet
SPERS_DIALOG	Edit Personalization
SPERS_MAINT	Personalization object processing
SPERS_REUSE_DEMO	Personalization Test Transaction
SPERS_TEST	Test personalization objects
SPH1	Create and maintain telephony server
SPH2	Maintain outgoing number change
SPH3	Maintain incoming number change
SPH4	Activ./deactiv. telephony in system
SPH5	Define address data areas
SPH6	Language-dependent server descrip.

SPH7	Language-dep. addr. data area texts
SPHA	Telephony administration
SPHB	SAPphone: System Administration
SPHD	SAPphone: Own telephone number
SPHS	SAPphone: Interface for Telephone
SPHSREMOTE	Start Softphone remote
SPHT	SAPphone Test Environment
SPHW	Initiate Call in Web Applications
SPIA	PMI Administration
SPIC	Spool installation check

ST01	System Trace
ST11	Display Developer Traces
ST14	Application Analysis
ST20	Screen Trace
ST20LC	Layout Check
ST4A	Database: Shared cursor cache (ST04)
ST62	Create Industry Short Texts
STARTING_URLS	SMTR_NAVIGATION_SEND_MESSAGE
START_AGR_GENERATOR	Adjust all SAP roles
START_REPORT	Starts report
STAV_TABR	Settle - Status Management
STCTRL_COPY	Copy Table Control User Settings
STCUP	Table control variants upgrade
STDC	Debugger output/control

STDR	Object Directory Consistency Check
STDU	Debugger display/control (user)
STEMPLATE	Customizing templates
STEMPMERGE	Mix templates
STEP10	Export STEP Data
STEP20	Import STEP Data
STERM	SAPterm Terminology Maintenance
STERM_EXTERNAL	Transaction STERM: External Callup
STERM_KEYWORDS	Maintain Index Entries
STERM_REMOTE	Transaction STERM: RFC Callup
STFB	CATT function module test
STFO	Plan Service Connection
STI1	Change Documents Payment Details
STI2	Change Docs Correspondence
STI3	Chg. Docs Transaction Authoriz.
STKONTEXTTRACE	Switch On Context Trace
STMA	Proposal Pool Administration
STMP	Proposal Pool: Selection
STPD	Test Workbench
STRUST	Trust Manager
STRUSTSSO2	Trust Manager for Logon Ticket
STSEC	Maintain events deadline

	segment
STSEC_DLV	Maintain events deadline segment
STSEC_TRA	Maintain events deadline segment
STSN	Customizing Number Ranges Time Strm
STSSC	Maintain deadline procedures
STSSC_DLV	Maintain shipping deadline procedure
STSSC_TRA	Maintain transportation dline proc.
STSTC	Maintain times in time segment
STSTC_DLV	Maintain times in time segment
STSTC_TRA	Maintain times in time segment
STTO	Test Organization
STVARV	Selection variable maint. (TVARV)
STZAC	Maintain time zone act. in client
STZAD	Disp.time zone activat.in client
STZBC	Maintain time zones in Basis Cust.
STZBD	Display time zones (Basis Cust.)
STZCH	Time zones: Consistency checks
STZEC	Time zone mapping in ext.

	systems
STZED	Time zone mapping in ext. systems
STZGC	Time zones: Maintain geo.data
STZGD	Time zone cust.: Disp.geo.data
SE16	Data Browser
SE16N	General Table Display
SE16_ANEA	Data Browser ANEA
SE16_ANEK	Data Browser ANEK
SE16_ANEP	Data Browser ANEP
SE16_ANLA	Data Browser ANLA
SE16_ANLC	Data Browser ANLC
SE16_ANLP	Data Browser ANLP
SE16_ANLZ	Data Browser ANLZ
SE16_BKPF	Data Browser BKPF
SE16_BSEG	Data Browser BSEG
SE16_BSID	Data Browser BSID
SE16_BSIK	Data Browser BSIK
SE16_BSIS	Data Browser BSIS
SE16_ECMCA	Data Browser Journal Entries
SE16_ECMCT	Data Browser Totals Records
SE16_KNA1	Data Browser KNA1
SE16_KNB1	Data Browser KNB1
SE16_LFA1	Data Browser LFA1
SE16_LFB1	Data Browser LFB1
SE16_MARA	Data Browser MARA
SE16_MARC	Data Browser MARC

SE16_RFCDESSECU	Data Browser RFCDESSECU
SE16_SKA1	Data Browser SKA1
SE16_SKB1	Data Browser SKB1
SE16_T000	Data Browser T000
SE16_T807R	Data Browser T807R
SE16_TCJ_CHECK_STACK	Data Browser TCJ_CHECK_STACKS
SE16_TCJ_CPD	Data Browser TCJ_CPD
SE16_TCJ_C_JOURNALS	Data Browser TCJ_C_JOURNALS
SE16_TCJ_DOCUMENTS	Data Browser TCJ_DOCUMENTS
SE16_TCJ_POSITIONS	Data Browser TCJ_POSITIONS
SE16_TCJ_WTAX_ITEMS	Data Browser TCJ_WTAX_ITEMS
SE16_TXCOMSECU	Data Browser TXCOMSECU
SE16_USR40	Data Browser USR40
SE16_USRACL	Data Browser USRACL
SE16_USRACLEXT	Data Browser USRACLEXT
SE16_V_T599R	Data Browser V_T599R
SE16_W3TREES	Data Browser W3TREES
SE16_WWWFUNC	Data Browser WWWFUNC
SE16_WWWREPS	Data Browser WWWREPS
SE17	General Table Display
SE18	Business Add-Ins: Definitions
SE18_OLD	Business Add-Ins: Definitions (Old)
SE19	Business Add-Ins: Implementations

SE19_OLD	Business Add-Ins: Implementations
SE38P	Delete ALE Change Pointers
SE38Q	Init. Data Transfer In Transit Qty
SE39	Splitscreen Editor: (New)
SE39O	Splitscreen Editor: Program Compare
SE40	MP: Standards Maint. and Translation
SE61	R/3 Documentation
SE61D	Display of SAPScript Text
SE62	Industry Utilities
SE63	Translation: Initial Screen
SE63_OTR	Translation - OTR
SE64	Terminology
SE71	SAPscript form
SE72	SAPscript Styles
SE73	SAPscript Font Maintenance
SE74	SAPscript format conversion
SE75	SAPscript Settings
SE75TTDTGC	SAPscript: Change standard symbols
SE75TTDTGD	SAPscript: Display standard symbols
SE76	SAPscript: Form Translation
SE77	SAPscript Styles Translation
SE78	Administration of Form Graphics
SE80	Object Navigator
SE81	Application Hierarchy

SE82	Application Hierarchy
SE83	Reuse Library
SE83_START	Start Reuse Library
SE84	R/3 Repository Information System
SE85	ABAP/4 Repository Information System
SE89	Maintain Trees in Information System
SE8I	Lists in Repository Infosystem
SE90	Process Model Information System
SE91	Message Maintenance
SE92	New SysLog? Msg Maintenance as of 46A
SE92N	Maintain System Log Messages
SE93	Maintain Transaction Codes
SE94	Customer enhancement simulation
SE95	Modification Browser
SE95_UTIL	Modification Browser Utilities
SE97	Maintain transaction call authorization
SEARCH_SAP_MENU	Find in SAP Menu
SEARCH_USER_MENU	Find in User Menu
SECATT	Extended Computer Aided Test Tool
SECOCO	Control Composer
SECR	Audit Information System

SECSTO	Administration of Secure Memory
SELVIEW	Selection view maintenance
SEM_BEX	Business Explorer Analyzer
SEM_NAV	Business Explorer Navigator
SENG	Administration of External Indexes
SENGEXPLORER	Explorer Index Administration
SEO_PATTERN_GENE RATE	Update Pattern
SERP	Reporting: Change Tree Structure
SESS	Session Manager Menu Tree Display
SESSION_MANAGER	Session Manager Menu Tree Display
SESS_START_OBJECT	Start an Object
SEU_DEPTYPE	Maintain dependency types
SEU_INT	Object Navigator

Index

Please visit www.sapcookbook.com to read more about other books in our SAP Interview Questions, Answers, and Explanations series:

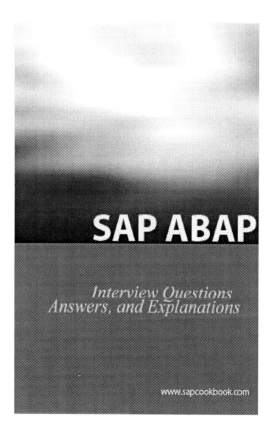

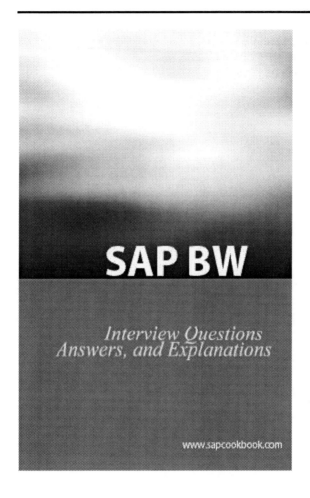

Lightning Source UK Ltd.
Milton Keynes UK
UKOW04f0515200214

226821UK00001B/41/A